Rolf Heimann's BIZARRE BRAIN BENDERS

Watermill Press

First published in USA by Watermill Press

First published by Periscope Press, a division of Roland Harvey Studios, Australia, 1992

Designed by Matt Kennedy

Printed in USA

ISBN 0 8167 3035 0

10 9 8 7 6 5 4 3 2 1

Bizarre Blurb

What is the single most important factor in making an Olympic athlete a top class competitor? Ask any of them and I'll bet they say, "Practice." They must repeat their event over and over until they do it to the best of their ability.

So, it makes sense that to keep your brain in top condition, you should give it a good workout as often as possible. That's why I have written this book, *Bizarre Brainbenders*. **I hope you have fun on your way through – but try not to look at the answers! But just in case you have to look, they start on page 29. Best of luck!**

1

El Magnifico is about to perform his best magic trick – pulling thirteen white rabbits from his top hat. But how embarrassing! Not a single rabbit appears!

Can you find El Magnifico's rabbits?

2 Captain Whalebone's buried treasure

This is a page from Captain Whalebone's diary:

We dropped anchor in a little bay and set out immediately to find a good hiding place for our gold. We walked through swampy ground towards a distant peak, which I called Mount Whalebone. Soon we crossed a small creek which I named Whalebone River. Not long after that we came across a smelly lake, which I called Schnock's Pond, after my first mate. The miserable stream that flowed into it I called Schnock's Creek. Following the creek upstream we discovered a magnificent waterfall, which I named Whalebone Falls. Here is where we buried the treasure, by the light of the sinking sun, right in the shadow of a large rock above Whalebone Falls. Then we walked back to the ship in Whalebone Bay.

Looking at the old map, can you work out where the treasure is buried, and the location of Whalebone Bay?

Tile tangle

Time limit: 45 seconds

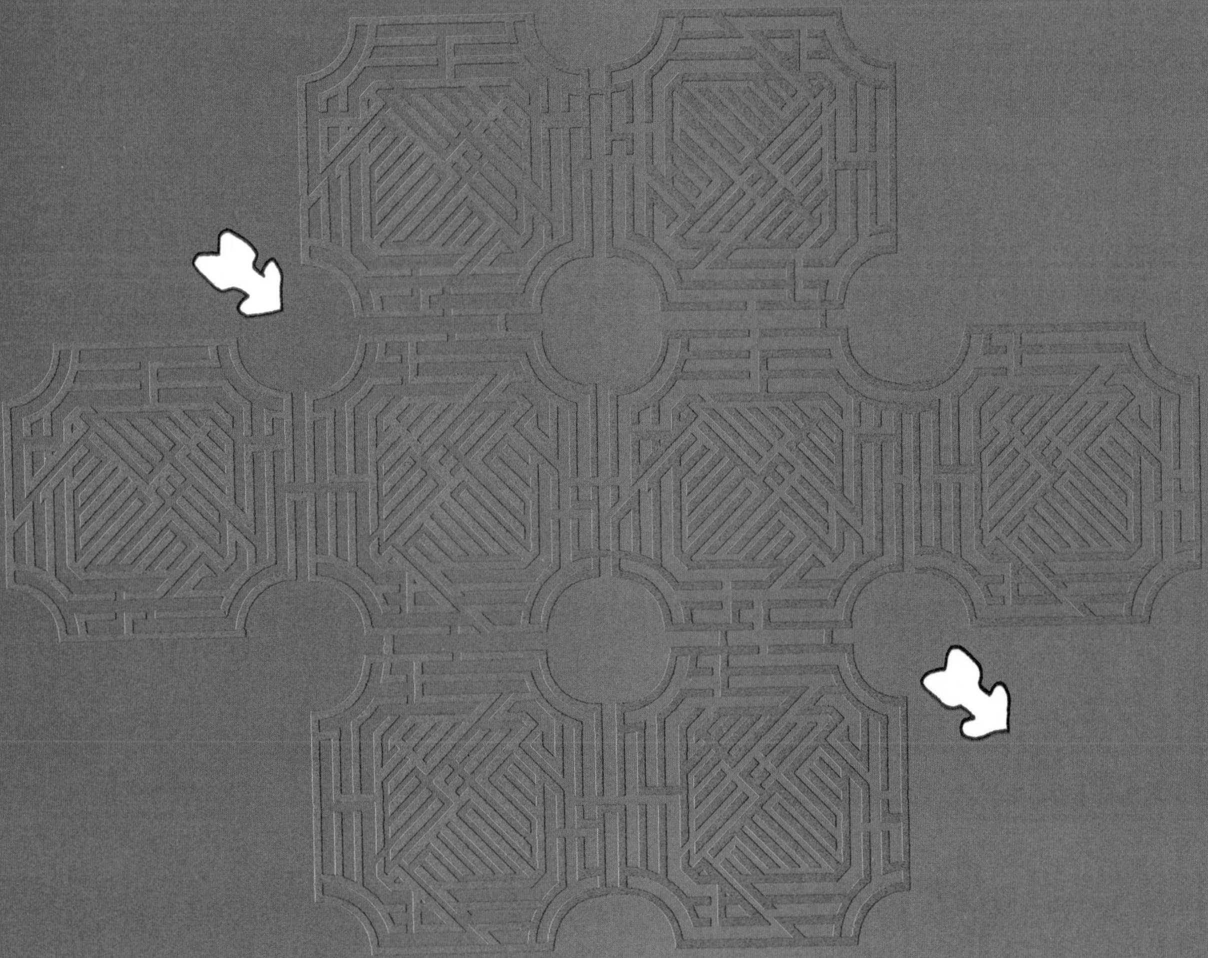

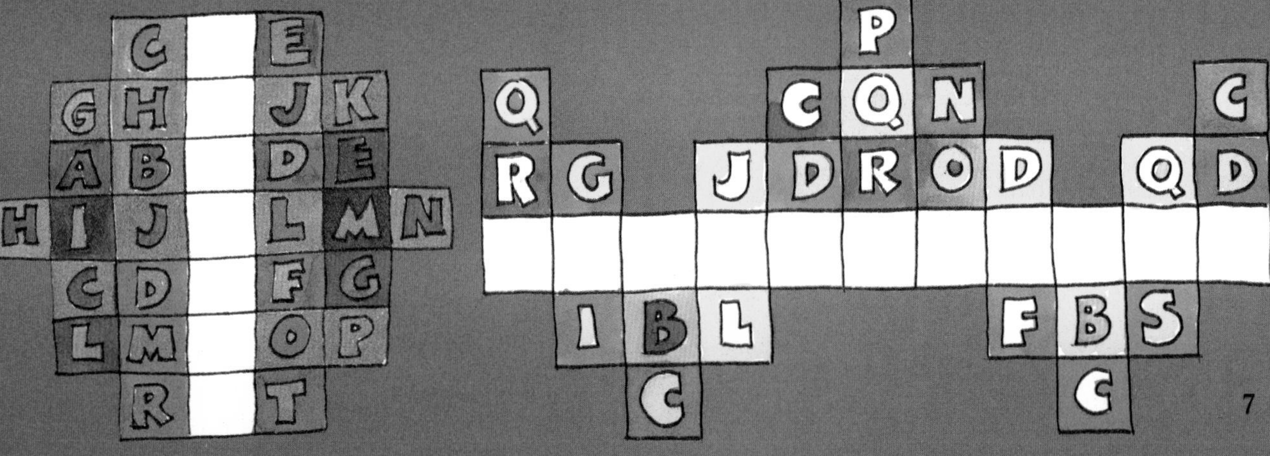

Fill in the missing letters, and find the name of two English writers. But first you must crack the code! (Clue: How well do you know your alphabet?)

INDIANS
COLUMBUS LANDING
ANNE

5

Columbus capers

"Cut!" screamed film director Schomirroff. "What is the meaning of this? Where is Anne? Isn't she responsible for getting the right props for this scene? Columbus would not have worn shoes like this! This is supposed to be the year 1492, when Columbus discovered America."

The shoe is not the only thing that is wrong with the scene. There are at least twelve others that you may be able to find.

Round the twist in 60 seconds

Time limit: one minute.

Microchip mayhem

Time limit: this one should take only 30 seconds!

Problem panels

What do these panels have in common?

All for one and one for all

Each of these panels could be considered the odd one out. Can you work out why?

4 SALE
15
SOLICITOR
1

10 Magpie mayhem

This whole town seems to be falling apart! A smug-looking magpie is stealing anything it can gets its beak around. Can you find where all the items in its nest have come from?

By the way, many of the townsfolk have dogs to scare the magpie away. How many dogs can you spot?

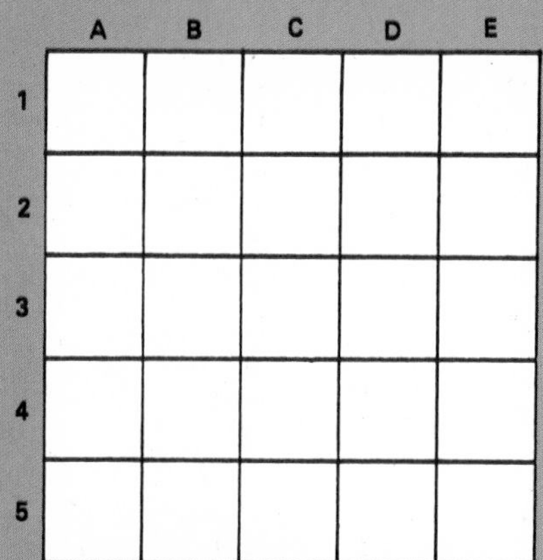

Jigsaw jumble

By transferring the jumbled lines in the left-hand grid to the correct place in the right-hand grid, you should be able to form the picture.

Double trouble

A two-headed snake? That is something to see! Unfortunately it has been released into the normal snakepit and is very difficult to find . . .

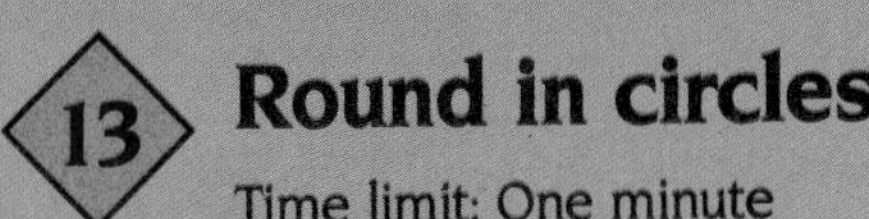

13 Round in circles

Time limit: One minute

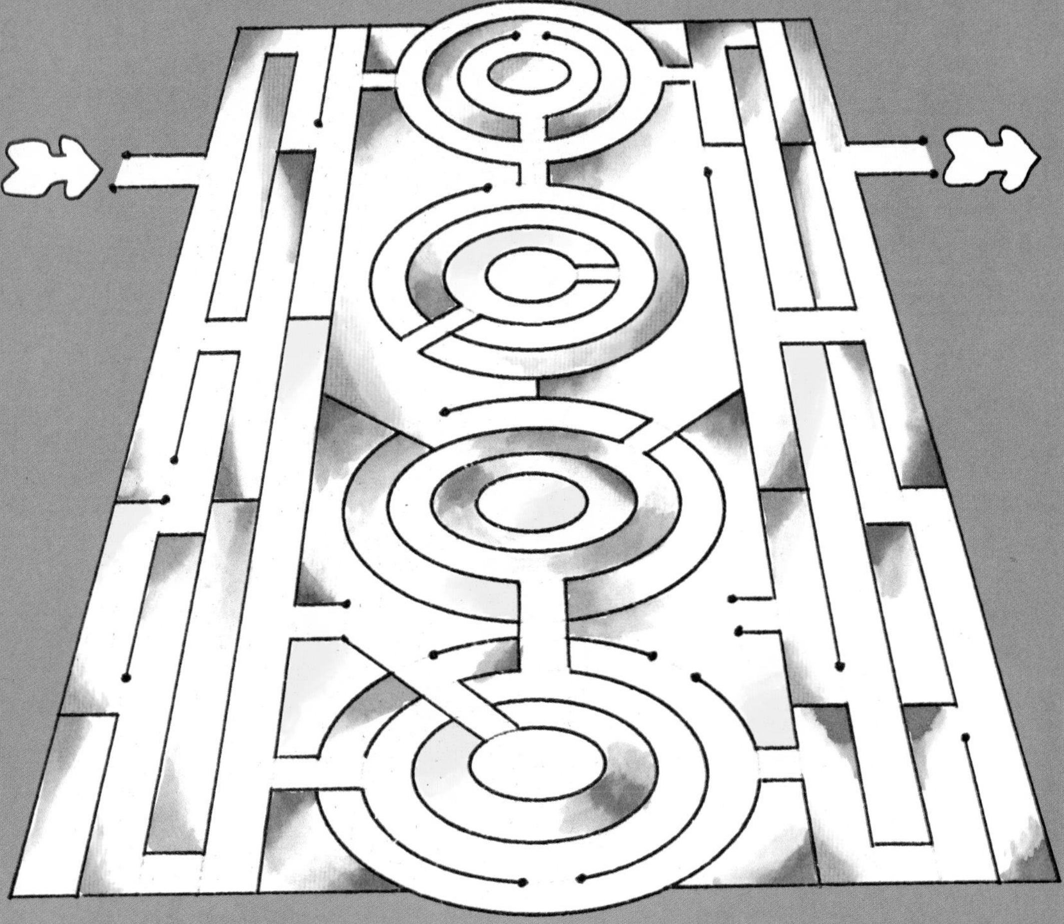

14 Dots with a difference

Follow the alphabet – and don't be confused by the numbers!

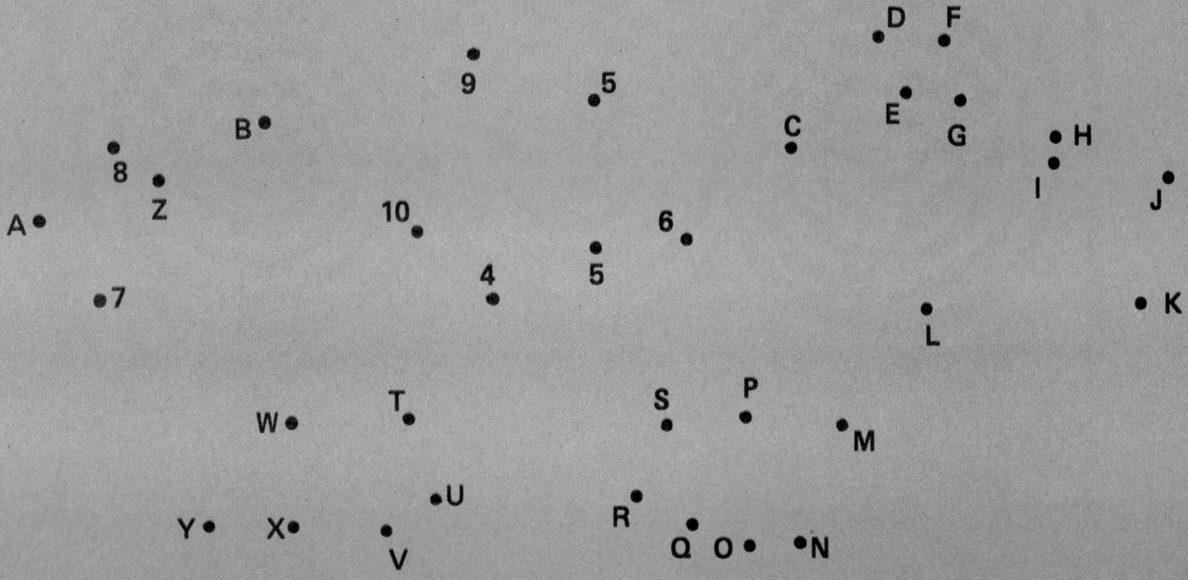

15 Face to face with painting

Alberto Chiaroscuro, the famous portrait painter, went out in search of a person to paint. He much preferred painting faces to painting landscapes,

but as much as he looked he could not find a person to sit for him. Luckily his imagination saw faces in everything!

How many faces would he be able to see in this landscape? Don't forget to turn the page upside-down and sideways!

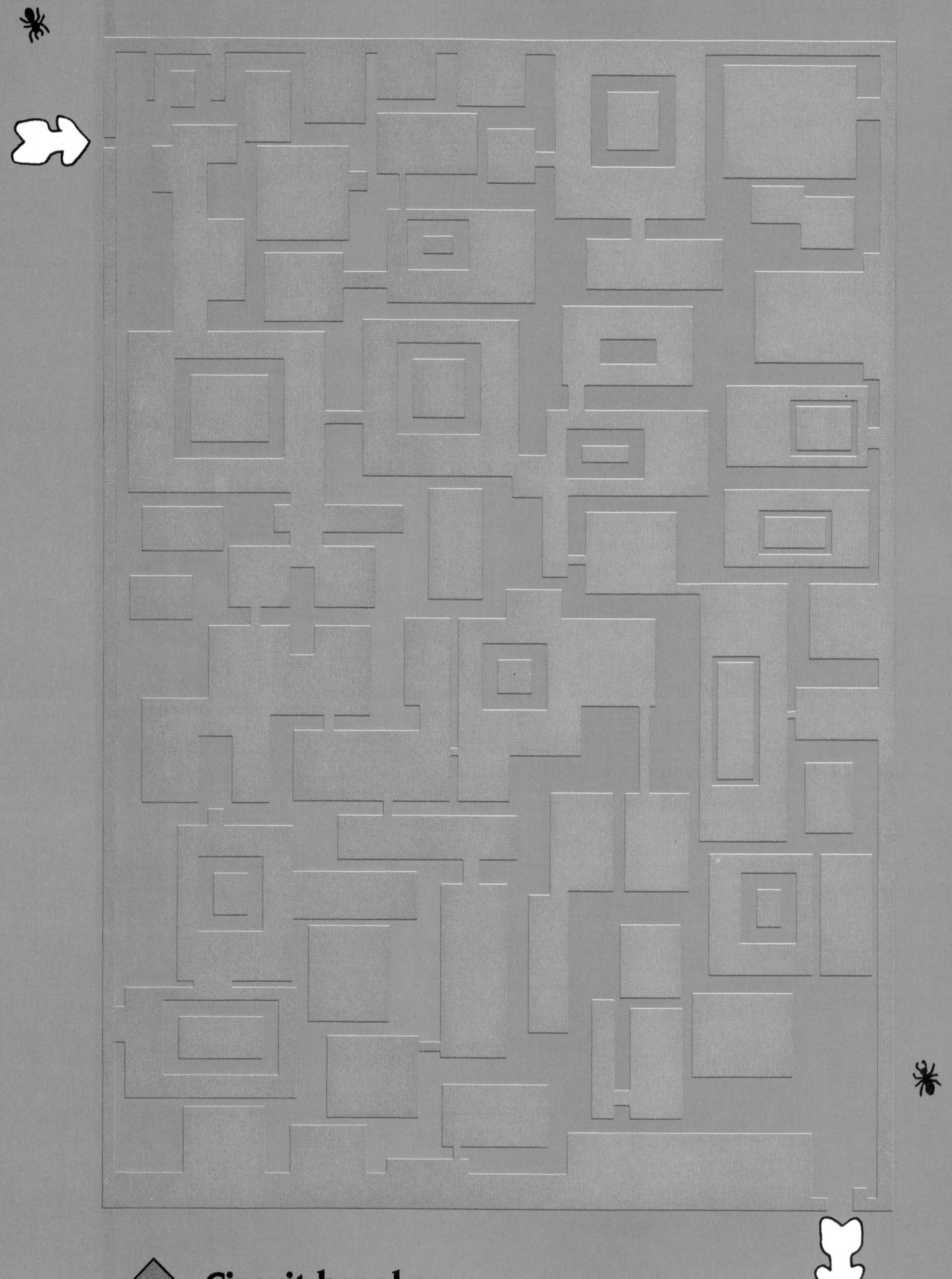

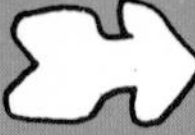

Circuit breaker

Time limit: 30 seconds

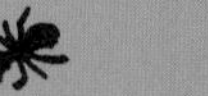

Capital idea!

The names of 14 international capital cities are hidden in this word puzzle. See how many you can find.

L	R	P	A	R	W	A	M	C	B
I	O	O	T	T	A	W	A	A	U
M	M	N	I	L	S	C	D	N	D
A	E	P	D	F	H	W	R	B	A
P	O	L	S	O	I	K	I	E	P
B	E	R	L	I	N	C	D	R	E
L	O	P	R	A	G	U	E	R	S
G	S	N	E	H	T	A	C	A	T
L	N	A	I	R	O	B	I	P	L
W	E	L	L	I	N	G	T	O	N

Amazing ant-ics

There is turmoil at the ant farm! The old queen just got sick of her job, so she abdicated. The ant that first reaches the royal chamber will be crowned the new queen.

Which entrance leads to the royal chamber?

19
Zany zoo
What a shock! During the night, someone stole the zookeeper's keys and opened all the cages. He'll need some help to find all the animals: 8 monkeys, 8 snakes, 6 penguins, 5 turtles, 4 seals, 3 bears, 1 camel, 2 giraffes, 1 elephant and 1 kangaroo.

ELEPHANT
KANGAROO
PENGUINS
BEARS
SNAKES
ZOO

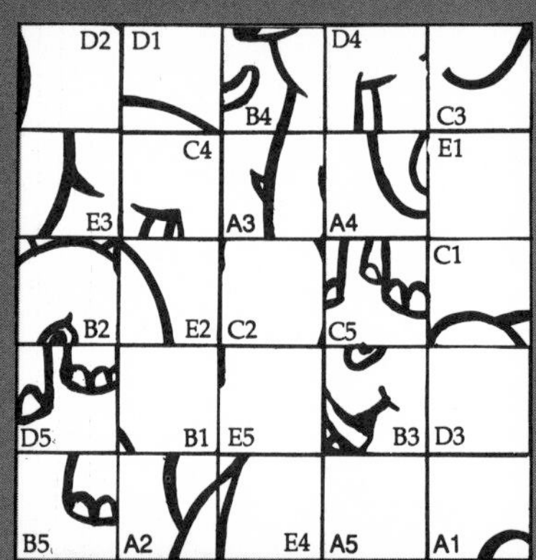

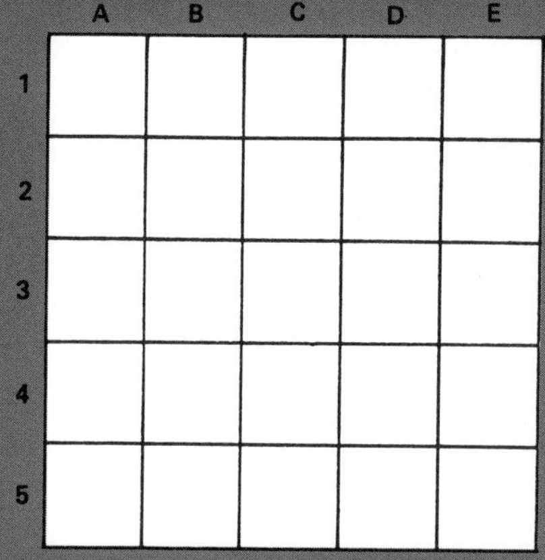

20 Jumbo jumble

By transferring the jumbled lines in the left-hand grid to the correct place in the right-hand grid, you should be able to form the picture.

21 Six-sided similarity

Make your way through the hexagons by stepping from the first panel to the one that shares some similarity. For example, pear to apple, apple to pumpkin . . .

Model city

Ella Gesson is the new fashion model for Highlife magazine. Everybody wonders where she comes from. You can find out by taking the letters from the left and putting them in a new order on the right.

E L L A G E S S O N

Bubble burster

Time limit: 30 seconds

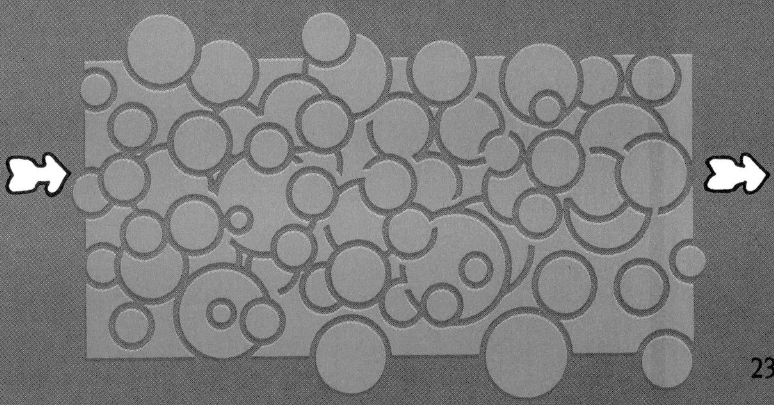

53
BUTCHER
58
Florist
57
TOILETS
IN
OUT
ONE WAY
VISIT
LONDON
PIANO
RECITAL
by
MOHAMME
ALI

24
Oddsville
"Casa Pepe – that's the oddest name for a Chinese restaurant that I've ever seen!" said Mr. Gibson.
"Not as odd as the food they seem to serve," remarked his wife. "In fact this must be the oddest town we've ever visited! Just look around!"
Mrs. Gibson was right. The town was full of odd and crazy things – and even some things that were absolutely impossible. Can you spot them?
RED
CASA PEPE
Chinese Restaurant
Today's Special:
Sauerkraut a la Astronaut
with
Chocolate Gumbo!!!!
No Smoking
Restaurant

25 Dreaded diagonals

Time limit: this one is easier than it looks – no more than 45 seconds!

Hidden fame

The names of seventeen famous men of history are hidden in the word puzzle. See how many you know.

E	I	N	S	T	E	I	N	E	R
L	R	L	L	E	B	H	L	C	E
L	O	F	E	M	N	C	O	O	K
I	R	P	S	O	O	A	C	L	L
H	E	A	E	Z	E	B	N	U	N
C	H	S	I	A	L	P	I	M	O
R	T	T	D	R	O	F	L	B	S
U	U	E	R	T	P	A	S	U	I
H	L	U	E	W	A	T	T	S	D
C	E	R	V	A	N	T	E	S	E

27

Isn't it amazing how many butterflies there are in the world? Some may look similar, but, on close inspection, are different in some small way.

Find a butterfly that matches the one on the poster – right down to the last spot!

Crazy cogs

Time limit: 45 seconds

Detective McQuick was on the track of two bank robbers. One of them had already escaped overseas and had left a note for his accomplice telling him where he had gone. The note was written in a strange code, but it took only five minutes for Detective McQuick to work out the name of the city.

How long will it take you?

The Answers

Here are the solutions to the more difficult brainbenders.

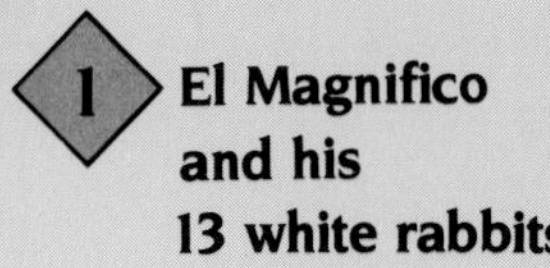

1 El Magnifico and his 13 white rabbits

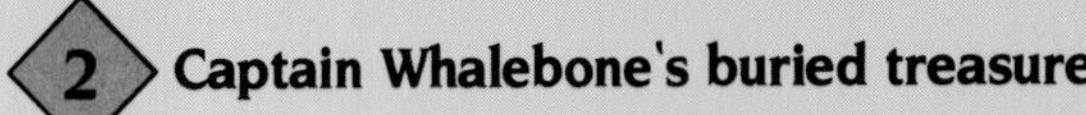

2 Captain Whalebone's buried treasure

3 Tile tangle

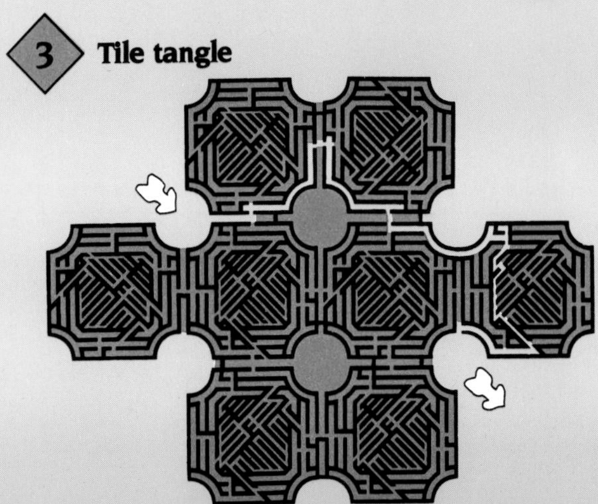

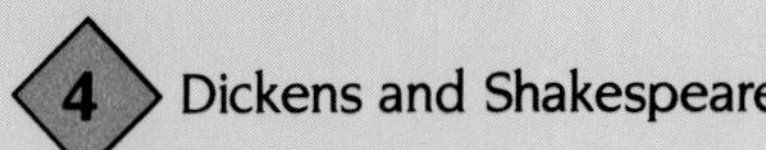

4 Dickens and Shakespeare

5 Columbus capers
When Columbus landed on American shores, there were no paddlesteamers, no lighthouses, no flag of the USA, no revolvers, no sunglasses, no cameras, no outboard engines, no wristwatches, no baseball caps. Also, tobacco pipes were unknown to Europeans and American Indians did not have T-shirts, firearms, horses, or thongs.

8 Problem panels
The number 4 is common to each panel – 4 dots, 4 masts, 4 legs...

9 All for one and one for all
The first panel is the only one containing red, the second panel shows the only living thing, the third panel has the only yellow background and the fourth panel shows the only object that has nothing to do with water.

10 Magpie mayhem

There are seven dogs.

11 Jigsaw jumble

12 Double trouble

The two-headed snake is the one straight down from the boy's hand at left.

14 Dots with a difference

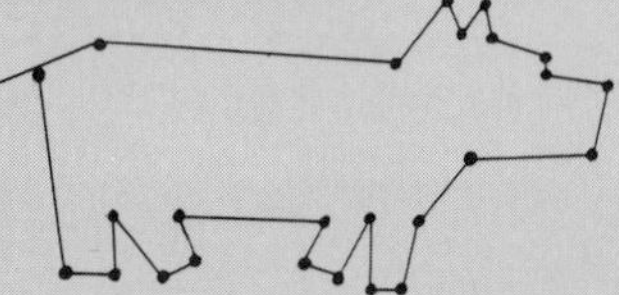

15 Face to face with painting

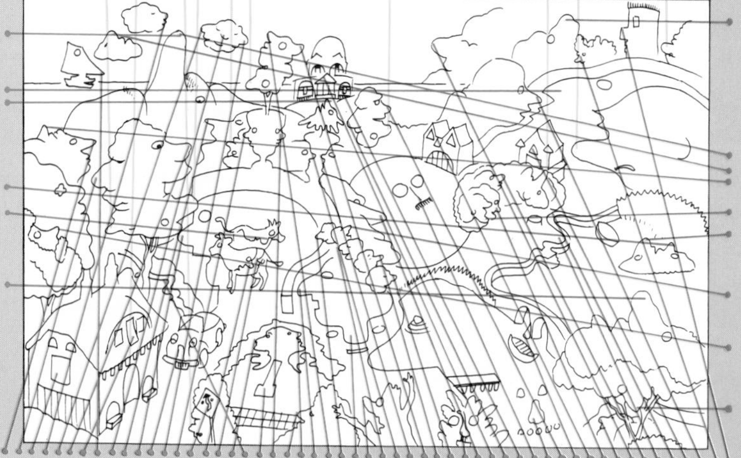

17 Capital idea!

The 14 international cities are:

Budapest	Ottawa
Madrid	Wellington
Washington	Canberra
London	Lima
Berlin	Oslo
Prague	Nairobi
Athens	Rome

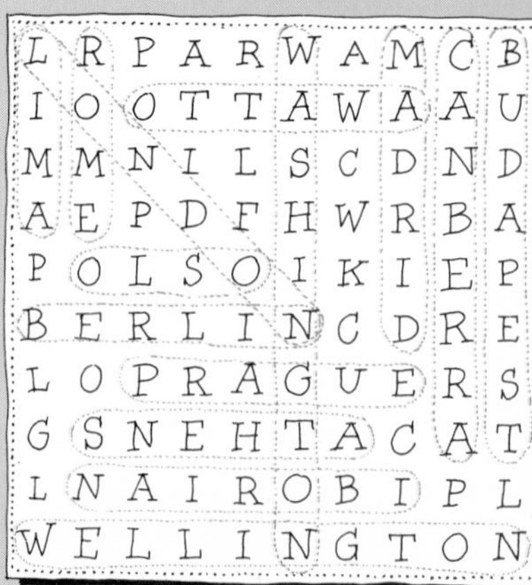

18 Amazing ant-ics

19 Zany zoo

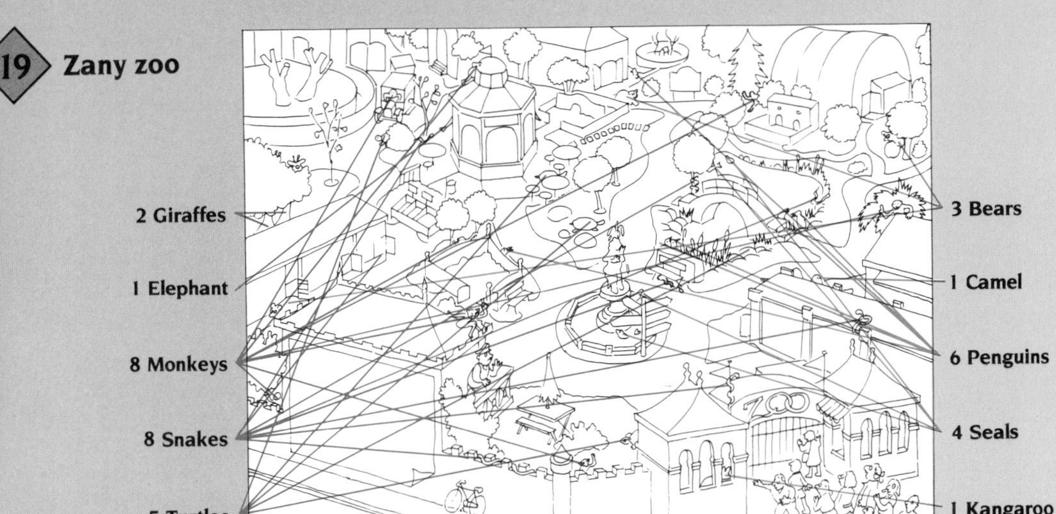

20 Jumbo jumble

21 Six-sided similarity

The correct sequence is: pear, apple, pumpkin, skull, bones, pirate ship, steamer, whale, fountain, watering can, seedling, tree, pear.

22 Model city

Ella Gesson comes from Los Angeles.

24 Oddsville

Here is a list of things that are wrong in Oddsville:

1. The Baker's shop is called "Butcher."
2. The street numbers are out of numerical order.
3. All three clocks show different times.
4. The exit door in the toilet block leads to the river.
5. The dog has 6 legs.
6. The traffic is traveling the wrong way down a one-day street.
7. The whip and the fishing rod have swapped places.
8. The poster saying "Visit London" shows the Eiffel Tower in Paris.
9. Mohammed Ali is famous for his boxing brilliance, not his piano recitals.
10. The horse pulling the cart has a cat's tail.
11. A hose leads from the water tap to a lamp.
12. The paddlesteamer could not have fit under the bridge.
13. The paddlesteamer's smoke is blown one way and the flag another.
14. The U.S. flag is incorrect.
15. The paddlesteamer's port light is red, and the starboard light is green (should be the other way around).
16. The chessboard should have 8 squares on each edge.
17. The man on the park bench is playing a cello that is shaped like a guitar.
18. The drainpipe on the balcony of the Casa Pepe restaurant leads to a wastepaper basket.
19. The man on the balcony is holding the telephone receiver upside-down.
20. The can of yellow paint is marked "Red."
21. A man is smoking a pipe in a non-smoking restaurant.
22. Two people are playing a game that is a combination of golf and badminton.

26 Hidden fame

The 17 famous men are:

Einstein	Bach
Churchill	Columbus
Pasteur	Napoleon
Luther	Cook
Cervantes	Edison
Steiner	Ford
Verdi	Bell
Diesel	Watt
Mozart	

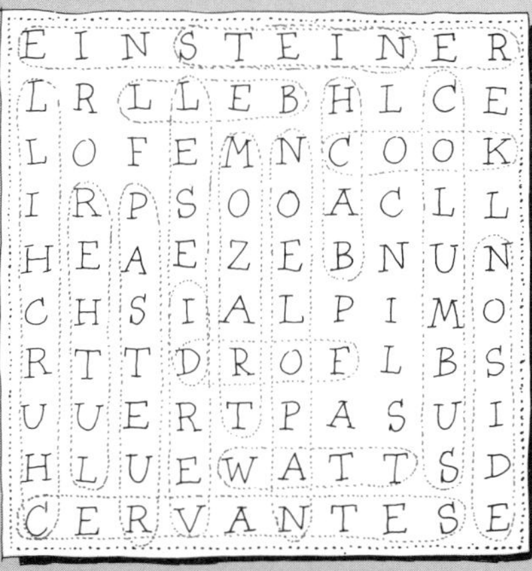

27 Here is the matching butterfly:

29 Detective McQuick

If you cover the lower half of the strange letters you can read "Rio De Janeiro."

And finally, bend your brain around this one!